The Perfect Pumpkin

Kristin Rene

AuthorHouse™
1663 Liberty Drive
Bloomington, IN 47403
www.authorhouse.com
Phone: 1 (800) 839-8640

Published by AuthorHouse 12/10/2016

ISBN: 978-1-5246-5302-6 (sc)

Library of Congress Control Number: 2016919916

Print information available on the last page.

authorHOUSE®

To my family,

Because I was afraid,

I say thank you for believing in me.

Because I was lazy,

I say thank you for motivating me.

And because it comes from my heart,

I hope you enjoy.

Most children get excited when at the pumpkin patch.

They run and look for the perfect one to snatch.

They shout,

"It must be orange!"

"And round at its feet!"

Because that's the type of pumpkin most
children want to meet.

"It must be tall!"

"And a great deal wide!"

Never stopping to think about what is on the inside.

They run and approach the *best* of the *best*.

Giving them the awards of Pumpkins Best Dressed.

All the pumpkins stood proudly waiting to be picked.

Hoping when they are snatched up they are not being tricked.

The great pumpkins scream,

"Pick me!"

"Pick me!"

But the littlest pumpkin was just too little to see.

All the pumpkins found homes, except for just one,

The little orange runt, green and spotted from the sun.

A school bus had come and no one had bought,

The small little pumpkin left all alone to rot.

But along came a child with something special within,

She cared not for the coolest round pumpkin to win.

She looked all around as the children went wild,

But a green spotted light caught the eye of this child.

She found the runt pumpkin and started to see

His spots were like freckles adding personality!

She walked with her new friend to the front to pay.

When a few little kids decided they had something to say.

"What is that thing?"

"Why isn't he orange like mine?"

"I happen to think his spots are lovely and are one of a kind."

She defended her new friend and walked off the lot

Knowing she picked the best pumpkin out of the whole spot.

Because it's not about looking like everyone around,

It's about being yourself that truly makes the loudest sound.

About the Author

Kristin Rene is a passion fueled adventure seeker whose love for story telling began at a very early age. Her interests focus largely around human connection and self motivation.

You can find her traveling the globe, doodling on napkins, or singing show tunes on any given day. She currently lives in southern California. Visit www.amermaidstail.net to learn more about her creative chaos.